HERMAN®

VOLUME 1

CLASSICS

Published by ECW PRESS
2120 Queen Street East, Suite 200, Toronto, Ontario, Canada M4E 1E2

For HERMAN® permissions, licensing information,
and other product information, contact:
LaughingStock Licensing Inc.
P.O. Box 3006, Station C,
Ottawa, Ontario, Canada K1Y 4J3
(www.laughingstock.com)

HERMAN comics are distributed to newspapers worldwide by
United Media, 200 Madison Avenue, New York, NY, U.S.A. 10016

NATIONAL LIBRARY OF CANADA CATALOGUING IN PUBLICATION

Unger, Jim
Herman Classics / Jim Unger.
ISBN:1-55022-616-9 (v. 1)
I. Title.
NC1449.U48A4 2003   741.5'971   C2003-904330-4

DISTRIBUTION

CANADA: Jaguar Book Group, 100 Armstrong Avenue, Georgetown, Ontario, L7G 5S4

UNITED STATES: Independent Publishers Group, 814 North Franklin
Street, Chicago, Illinois 60610

PRINTED AND BOUND IN CANADA

HERMAN

— VOLUME 1 —

CLASSICS

by JIM Unger

ECW Press

"Got any books on dog training?"

Meeting Jim Unger

by David Waisglass

Few things made my mother laugh as loudly as HERMAN. Every morning she would snicker, giggle, and guffaw as she snipped the latest installment of HERMAN from our newspaper. By the time the first HERMAN book was published in 1979, her faded mementos had grown into an unruly pile in our kitchen.

It seemed everyone soon owned a best-selling HERMAN book, with millions of fans quickly reciting their favorite gags with little prompting. In fact, each comic was so hilariously imaginative, it inspired a new generation of creators including Gary Larson (THE FAR SIDE), Dave Coverly (SPEED BUMP), Steve Moore (IN THE BLEACHERS), Scott Adams (DILBERT), and numerous others.

When I created my own syndicated newspaper comic (FARCUS) in 1990, the comparisons to Jim Unger's work were inevitable.

"It's OK, Mom. I know you like HERMAN better than FARCUS."

"That's not true!" she would argue. "I love your work."

"Yeah? Which one is your favorite?"

"The one with the cowboy who has arrows in his back, and says 'My arthritis. It's cured!'"

That *was* a HERMAN comic, but I didn't mind. I knew Jim Unger had set the bar very high.

As I walked down the hallowed Hall of Fame at Universal Press Syndicate to sign my first contract, I stopped before a larger-than-life photo of a wild-haired man in a city park mischievously grinning as he groped the bare-breasted statue of a woman. "That's Jim," said the syndicate vice-president rolling his eyes. "I understand you met him?" I had.

Two years earlier I flew to the Bahamas to meet the legendary creator. "Next time you're in Nassau, come and visit," was all the encouragement I needed. Within minutes after hanging up the phone, I booked the flight and was on my way.

I had only recently begun self-syndicating my comic to a few dozen newspapers, when a mutual business acquaintance offered me Jim's private telephone number and suggested I meet him. "Funny you're both from Ottawa, Canada. You should meet him!"

"Maybe I will," I said as I wrote down the number, but there was no doubt about it.

For years I had studied and deconstructed his work — as I had done with many other humorists. Jim was undoubtedly master of the visual gag. Each panel portrayed an outrageous story of what has happened, or what is about to happen. With a unique illustrative style and an economy of line, Unger presented the funniest imaginable characters with truthful accuracy. But what makes HERMAN particularly hilarious is the characteristic wry response to repressed seething rage, bizarre circumstances, or perhaps a doomed fate.

I wanted to learn more about how Jim Unger worked, who he was, and perhaps catch a glimpse of what life may be like as a syndicated newspaper cartoonist.

Jim greeted me outside the hotel in a rusty Jeep, sporting a Tilley hat, white khakis, and photographer's vest. He looked more like a war-correspondent than a cartoonist and welcomed me as an old friend. Jim charmed everyone that way.

It seemed important to Jim that everyone liked him. And everyone did. He was quick with a smile or laugh. And always had time to get to know the waiter, grocery

Jim studies a HERMAN sculpture created by Canadian artist Keith Sandulak.

clerk, and gas attendant. People waved as we drove down the street. In Nassau, few people knew HERMAN, but everyone knew Jimmy. Jim tipped excessively, handing out money to almost anyone he thought needed it. He knew many of them personally, and talked compassionately about their troubled lives. "Poor kid. He's got AIDS," he'd say with his Londoner accent.

Everyone knew Jim to be sweet, loveable, spontaneous, child-like, trusting and, arguably, naïve. He had no interest in business or money. It bored him. One senior executive at Clement Communications said their team flew to Nassau to propose an enormously lucrative license to use HERMAN comics. As the CEO explained the workplace poster business, Jim could be heard snoring through the presentation.

Jim often entrusted his financial and business affairs to others who may have taken advantage of his easy-going nature. Although he was aware of some crooked dealings, he wasn't too concerned. "Karma," said Jim. "What goes around, comes around."

He was right. Things worked out well for Jimmy. He was living in Paradise as a world-famous cartoonist. Not bad for a poor kid who grew up on the tough streets of London and had numerous failed "careers" before discovering a talent for cartooning.

We drove to his beachside villa, where I met Bob. Jim's brother had melted into an over-sized crescent-shaped leather sofa gazing at an enormous television screen. Behind him stood a picturesque window of a brilliant turquoise Caribbean Sea. Bob invited me to sit, and for the next several hours the three of us talked about anything and everything.

Since 1982, Bob has lived in an adjoining house and authored many of the HERMAN gags. And he has inspired many more. (Yes, he accidentally ate a slice of the pizza box.)

For Jim and Bob, this was the center of their universe. It was perfect, and Jim reveled in it. "Let's face it, Dave," he'd say. "Life is too short to stress about little things. You've got to simplify your life."

In 1979, HERMAN *is syndicated to hundreds of newspapers worldwide and the first book tops the bestseller lists. Jim (above) produces his daily comics from his kitchen table in Ottawa, Canada.*

Jim's lifestyle and homespun philosophy were compelling and I quickly became his prodigy. Over the next several years, I spent more and more time in Nassau sitting on the couch with mentors Jim and Bob. We would debate various issues, tell stories, and laugh. The television would usually remain on CNN, perhaps only to prompt the next discussion.

"Poor ol' Chris," sighed Jim, commenting on the wheelchair-bound story of Superman. "At least he can still watch TV."

"Oh, that's great comfort," I said sarcastically.

"It's better than being dead!" argued Jim, who then turned to Bob for support. "Would you rather watch TV or be DEAD?!"

Bob thought for a moment as he watched the next contestant spin the Wheel of Fortune; "Depends what's on."

I almost fell on the floor laughing while Bob, characteristically, remained dead-pan, barely acknowledging his joke.

Bobbie is famous for mumbling one-liners that keep everyone in stitches.

The streetwise kid from London joined the British military and retired after recovering from a serious head injury. It turned out that Bob was not a typical tough guy but a serious intellectual who consumes books on a variety of subjects.

Each visit to Nassau was much like the next. We would get off the sofa only for a brief swim in the pool, a visit to the Casino, and perhaps for conch chowder at a local beachside restaurant.

"Why do you bother looking at the menu? You're going to order the chowder, just as you always do."

Jim glanced over his glasses, slammed the menu shut, and ordered fish.

We returned back to Jim's house, and I inevitably began to get restless. "Let's go somewhere, do something different!" I demanded of the world's most successful couch potato.

"Everything you need is right here, Dave! I can travel anywhere in the world on the Discovery Channel without baggage, insects, or bad hotel rooms."

Having tea with parents Lilian and Jim. "I think we were talking about my haircut," says Jim.

Jim's self-imposed exile is not entirely by his own design. Although it is barely apparent to others, Jim endures frequent bouts of depression, anxiety, and migraines — a clinical disorder that plagues many of his family members, including his mother and brother. It is difficult to imagine how he produces a hit comic 365 days every year.

Despite his pain, Jim can find humor in most situations. Of course, he doesn't have to look very far. Jim's inner circle of family and friends are as original as any characters imaginable.

Sister Debbie, husband Danny, and their three children are undoubtedly the inspired HERMAN family. Their true-life experiences are no less hysterical. No one makes me laugh louder and harder than they do. Even Danny's sister Shirley is a laugh for her ability to butcher language. (Apparently, she broke the news to the family that "Lady Di was killed in a car accident with Jody Foster after being chased into a tunnel by Pavarotti!")

On a family vacation to Boston, Danny refused to pay to get on a tour bus. Instead, he followed the bus around town with the kids holding their heads out the windows to hear what the tour operator was saying.

Jim's life is also a rich source of material — a brief stint in the British army, a London policeman working on the docks, an insurance clerk, a repo-man (repossessing automobiles), bookkeeper, etc. In 1968, he immigrated to Canada and exaggerated his qualifications to obtain a job as a page-layout artist for the *Mississauga Times* — a weekly suburban newspaper outside Toronto. When the paper's political cartoonist was on vacation, Jim briefly filled in and earned three cartooning awards. A friend suggested he become "syndicated" and provided him with a list of American newspaper syndicates.

Jim knew nothing about the business, but submitted some samples to Universal Press Syndicate (UPS) because "they sounded big." They weren't. John McMeel made his sales calls from a one-room office on Fifth Avenue in New York, while partner Jim Andrews edited copy from his home in Kansas City. The young syndicate had just begun distributing a new college strip "Doonesbury" and an American Greeting Card comic entitled "Ziggy." ups's greatest asset was its eye for talent, and over the next several years discovered "Cathy," "The Far Side," "Calvin and Hobbes," "For Better Or For Worse," among other comic hits.

The syndication deal was signed in the summer of 1974, and Jim began laboring over his first batch of daily comics. The timing could not have been worse. Jim had filed a "missing persons" report after his wife failed to return home. When the police showed up at his door to explain that she had taken up with another man, Jim still managed to meet the first of many comic deadlines with tears on the page.

It wasn't Jim's first marriage. As a young man in the army, Jim was briefly married, which he describes as "World War I." With his second marriage in the toilet, and an emerging new career as a cartoonist, Jim moved back to Ottawa where his parents, brother, and sisters resided.

HERMAN was an instant media success, but the 40-year-old celebrity was not entirely comfortable in the limelight. Mail arrived at his home in sacks. Television, radio, and magazine reporters all wanted interviews of the man who now hailed celebrity stardom befitting a rock-star. At book fairs, women would coyly hand him phone numbers, hotel keys, and even nude photographs of themselves. It was not something Jim had prepared for.

On one occasion, when asked to arrive early at a Chicago bookstore to sign copies of his first book, Jim stood outside in line with hundreds of other customers waiting for the store to open. He didn't realize they were waiting to see him.

Fame also brought scores of women to Jim's doorstep, and stories began to spread about the cartoonist's escapades. On an exhausting book fair and media tour circuit, Jim always found time to win the hearts of adoring fans. One of his college-aged conquests was the niece of a senior Syndicate executive, who later circulated warnings not to introduce Jim to family members.

"It wasn't what you might think," said Jim. "I really loved them. Every one of them was very special to me." No one could ever buy a bad line like that, but when Jim said it, I actually believed him. I still do.

Other than being able to more easily "pull in the birds," as Debbie calls it, success hadn't affected Jimmy. He bought a house for his parents, and lived in the upstairs apartment. There were also trips across the United States, Canada, and Europe. By 1982, Jim and Bob left the frigid Canadian winters for a beachside home in the Bahamas. And with the help of his brother, Jim continued to produce thousands of brilliant comics gags.

Although Jim's depression has caused him to retreat from the public eye, HERMAN has remained a top syndicated newspaper comic panel worldwide for almost 30 years.

It's humor that neither Jim nor Bob cares to analyze. "Its only purpose is to be funny," they say. But it's done exceptionally well. Enjoy.

David Waisglass is co-creator of the syndicated newspaper comic FARCUS *(www.farcus.com), distributed by Universal Press Syndicate from 1990 to 1997.*

Jim discovers his creative talents in 1972 when he fills in for a colleague at the
Mississauga Times *and produces several award-winning editorial cartoons.*

"I hate to mention it but there was a $1.80 on the meter when I hit that truck."

"He's weightlifting again."

"I make it a rule never to argue
about politics."

"What about our religious differences?
I worship money and you're broke!"

"How come I have to pay the same air
fare as a great lump like him?"

"Is that your idea of 20 pounds
of potatoes?"

"If I keep going to school, all the best
jobs are gonna be taken."

"You asleep AGAIN? I thought I told
you to count the sheep."

"It says here you're intelligent, honest
and reliable. What makes you think you'd
be an asset to this company?"

"As your former Latin professor, I can't
say you've exactly made my day."

"I see you taking a trip."

"If you insist on getting married,
I'm gonna break off our engagement."

"If a fool and his money are soon
parted, who's got yours?"

"Oh, 'elephants'! ... I thought you
said we're gonna cross the Alps
with 'elegance.'"

"What's with you ... don't you
like spaghetti?"

"As I remember, you always were
a big kid for your age."

"What do you mean, he's too noisy?"

"I'm not making any more cakes."

"It's hard to believe you've never put up wallpaper before."

"Sure, I'd love a second honeymoon ... who with?"

"I said 'I wanna marry your daughter when I get some money' and your father gave me twenty bucks."

"Another feature of this home is that it's within a stone's throw of several schools."

"Leave the car keys just in case something grabs you out there."

"Now you two! No fighting over the last cake."

"Now don't forget what the judge said about getting violent if you lose at cards."

"Stop whining. I caught it,
so I'll carry it."

"When I said I wanted a 'rare' steak,
I didn't mean one that took
two hours to find."

"You can't afford to get married on the
salary I'm paying you! One day you'll
thank me."

"Are you sure you're comfortable
like that?"

"That must have been one
heavy suitcase!"

"How long have these eggs
been in the fridge?"

"GET YOUR ELBOWS OFF THE TABLE!"

"Quit arguing and give
me my seven iron."

"Get up, you idiot. When I say, 'How do you
plead?' I wanna know if you're
'guilty' or 'not guilty.'"

"It'll take you a couple of days
to get used to them."

"No one said the job was going
to be easy!"

"Of course you never lose your ball ...
you never hit it more than a few feet."

"There's absolutely NOTHING on my
mind ... and anyway I don't want
to talk about it."

"Oh, darn!"

"Sounds like a power struggle between the spaghetti and the pickled onions."

"Wouldn't be your style to use a rolled-up newspaper, would it?"

"Want me to wrap it?"

"Your son-in-law's not here this afternoon. He's gone to your funeral."

"I want to leave you a tip but I haven't got change for a quarter."

"Sorry to keep you both waiting out here. Where's your wife?"

"They said he wasn't to leave the office 'til the books balanced."

HERMAN

JIM Unger

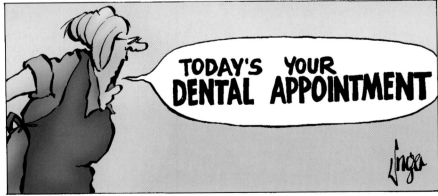

"Let me guess. She gave you your money back."

"I admire initiative, Watson, but when I say I want a 'funnel,' I mean one of these."

"Hey, it's good to see you again. That medicine must have worked last time!"

"Shove off. I'm sick of your jealousy!"

"Where do you get off taking
out your own appendix?"

"I'll run out and mortgage the house
and meet you at the checkout."

"PREPARE TO LOAD."

"Your nest egg just hatched."

"How are you getting on with the diet?"

"How am I supposed to make
the bed in the morning?"

"Hiya, Jonesy, you still watching
that 32-inch TV?"

"If I've gotta do typing and stuff like that, I want more money!"

"Sure you were good at history. You were there for most of it."

"The bank wants to lend us $5,000 to get out of debt!"

"You dropped it. You get it!"

"I'm gonna say my prayers.
D'you need anything?"

"How much longer did he tell you
to stay on this banana diet?"

"I have no way of knowing who started
this fight so I'm going to fine
you both $50."

"You mean I've gotta pay tax
on money I've already spent?"

"Did you win?"

"I wanna open a joint-account with someone who's got plenty of money."

"We've won a ten-percent discount on a round-the-world cruise."

"That new guy was supposed to be helping me roll this."

"I'm telling you; you don't have a complex. You ARE inferior."

"You wouldn't believe it, but some people press their tie BEFORE they put it on."

"The way you carry on, you'd think I enjoy these business trips."

"I appreciate this is your first day at the zoo, but from now on just paint the empty cages."

"Don't keep saying you don't like them. You've only had them on for 30 seconds."

"Where are the kids?"

"Haven't you got a brush?"

"It's just a simple little operation,
but we want you to pay now."

"I can do shorthand! It just
takes a little longer."

"You told me to save money,
so I got the economy size."

"That's why it didn't come back."

"I think he's trying to tell us
he can't paint!"

"Mom said we can get married and live
in the dining room if you don't mind
eating in the kitchen."

"We are now joining our regularly scheduled commercials which are already in progress."

"I tell you I saw its eyes move."

"LADIES AND GENTLEMEN, raise your glass to the bride and groom!"

"Give me a week's warning before they let you out of here and I'll clean the kitchen."

"If you're so dead set against gambling, how come you're in the marriage business?"

"Don't forget, I'm only practicing, so let me know if you feel anything."

"How could I have been doing 70 miles an hour when I've only been driving for ten minutes?"

"So that's your story, you 'hate to be late!'"

"Pretend you don't know you're on 'Candid Camera' and when I ask for a dime, give me five dollars."

"What happened? Did I touch a nerve?"

"Are you sure I'll be able to swim with it?"

"Our 'cupid computer' has come up with two names. Ghengis Khan and Attila the Hun."

"I don't care if it is plastic. I could have had a heart attack."

"Come in, Coach. I wanna discuss your lifetime contract."

"Your four aces don't beat two eights unless you have a red king with them!"

"Mr. Harrison took off for South America with the company payroll. Would you like to leave a message?"

"The man we're looking for must be dynamic
and aggressive."

"Sure it's faded! You've been wearing it during daylight hours without a jacket on."

"You've just turned this restaurant into a 'nonprofit' organization."

"You've still got your seatbelt on."

"Sure you can have it for ten bucks, but wouldn't you rather own a $200 painting?"

"If you were a horse,
we would have shot you!"

"I decided to come in today.
The poolroom's packed."

"Is this your first blind date?"

"Your jack slipped!"

"And another thing! I'm getting sick of you being so agreeable all the time."

"Who gets the triple 'jumbo-burger?'"

"... and when you take him out at night, try walking a bit faster."

"I was in the neighborhood and I thought I'd drop in for a couple of weeks."

JIM Unger

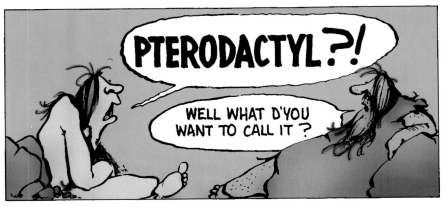

"Can you put my arm in a sling for
a couple of weeks so I can get out
of doing the dishes?"

"I don't mind the long wait;
the food here is terrible."

"Going ... going ..."

"The sporting goods store phoned.
You left your hat on the counter."

"No, I don't need help carrying it to the car. For $44, I need an armed guard."

"Don't worry about my punctuation. I'll be on time every morning."

"Whaddya making?"

"I know it's your first time in 38 years, but what would happen if everyone was ten minutes late for work?"

"Here, let me know if these work
and I'll give them a try myself."

"I wanted a steady worker, but you're
absolutely motionless."

"Hold it! They're out of season."

"STAMPEDE!"

"Try to relax."

"Shall I switch it off?"

"Mr. Henderson will see you now."

"Just take a seat, son. You're next."

"Have a good vacation. I've decided not to give you your bad news until you get back."

"You're supposed to say 'I do,' not 'I'll try.'"

"You've got six wives waiting for you on the outside. Are you sure you want parole?"

"Show me the paper again with
the calculations on it."

"Is that the only way you can
have a good time, smashing up
public property?"

"They said something about
five thousand UFOs landing in Idaho,
then cut to a commercial."

"Stay calm ... I'm gonna get a second
opinion on your blood pressure."

"Did you sleep okay, Herman?"

"You're the only guy we can trust in this cell 'til we get those bars fixed."

"I thought this stuff was supposed to attract girls."

"I went for my driving lesson and you owe them a new car."

"Sure it's big, but it'll do an average room in three minutes."

"As I see it, you've got a choice between a 'birdie' and promotion to branch manager."

"WAIST EIGHTY-TWO."

"Fifteen years up already?"

HERMAN

JIM Unger

DAD, CAN YOU LEND ME A DOLLAR?

WHY ARE YOU ALWAYS ASKING FOR MONEY?

WHEN I WAS YOUR AGE, I HAD TWO JOBS!

YOUR MOTHER AND I USED TO SAVE, EVEN AFTER WE GOT MARRIED!

WE MADE SACRIFICES. DIDN'T WE, HONEY?

A DOLLAR SAVED IS A DOLLAR EARNED.

YOU HAVE TO LEARN TO THINK AHEAD FOR A RAINY DAY.

WE'RE OVERDRAWN AT THE BANK AGAIN!

"Your wife took the baby home
an hour ago."

"I know there are a lot of things
more important than money and
they're all expensive!"

"Would you like me to conduct
one of your favorites?"

"I got fantastic references from
my last five jobs but I lost them on
the way over here."

"He wouldn't eat it so I put in some dirt and made it look like mud."

"When we get back I'm having you charged with mutiny."

"I don't care if it has got a bad leg. Get rid of it."

"You can take it off to have lunch."

"Mr. Henderson, he's written
another check!"

"I hope it tastes good. It's for the cat."

"Can't you ever get sick without
bringing home one of those?"

"The reason meat is expensive is
because no one ever argues with
a guy holding one of these."

"There, you left your toys all over the floor and now Mommy can't watch her favorite program."

"You may be sort of overqualified."

"I can't find my glasses."

"I see you've listed your hobbies as alpine skiing, scuba, sky-diving, treasure hunting and climbing Mount Everest."

"If you don't like the soup, just say so!"

"Congratulations! He seems very bright."

"Get off that oily man with your best shoes on."

"You must know how you got in there."

"Members of the jury, I ask you, does my client look like a man of violence?"

"They say opposites attract.
There must be plenty of good-looking,
intelligent girls around."

"Do I get to try again?"

"Look what your stupid uncle gave us.
What d'you think it is?"

"You're certainly enjoying my little cakes.
Have another one!"

"Judy, are you gonna elope
with me or not?"

"I found him working in the stockroom.
He's perfect!"

"The sink's backed up!"

"SLOW DOWN ... WATCH THAT
PUSSYCAT ... TURN RIGHT HERE."

"Writing your autobiography!
Who's it about?"

"Three nights in a row I've dreamt
you were Dracula."

"We can't live with my parents. They're
still living with their parents!"

"The way we treat a headache here is
to divert your attention to
something else."

"I take it you don't want any
of this cheese."

"Night work! You mean when it's dark?"

"Everyone in the building took up
a collection. Here's $225 for your violin."

"Don't look so miserable. Maybe the
first seven horses will be disqualified."

"Do you have any with more prickles?"

"I'll only be gone for a month,
so don't use the kitchen."

"I make it a rule never to lend money
to people who borrow!"

"He changed his mind about paying
the electricity bill."

"Will you get outta here with
that romantic junk!"

"I'll work my way up your arm and you
tell me when you feel anything."

"This is the third time in a week.
Why don't you wear a shirt?"

"There goes my tip, right?"

"I read somewhere that expensive
champagne doesn't go 'pop.'"

"You phoned me and said you had
amnesia; don't you remember?"

"If you don't learn a trade,
how are you going to know what
kind of work you're out of?"

"How many guys d'you know with
a solar-powered wristwatch?"

"… and if you marry her, how
do you intend to support us?"

"I saw that same look four years ago.
He's got a royal flush."

"I know I won't be losing a daughter.
YOU'LL be gaining a mother-in-law."

"He's got your hair!"

"No, no, no! Two is load ... THREE is fire!"

"Where did they get him from?"

"Madam, giving your husband 'twenty years in the slammer' is not my idea of a divorce settlement."

"I told you to use my insect spray."

"I'd ask for a doggie bag, but my dog
wouldn't eat that if I paid him."

"Did she tell you I got a job down
at the fish market?"

"Wanna see the list of extras?"

"Why don't you start climbing out
and I'll keep trying the buttons."

"It's called 'Pigeons Beware.'"

"Are you sure you're comfortable?"

"Is it still raining?"

"Don't forget to lock up when
you leave, Henderson."

HERMAN

JIM *Unger*

HEY, COME OVER HERE.

YOU'LL NEVER GUESS WHAT HAPPENS WHEN I RUB THESE STICKS TOGETHER!

I'VE INVENTED **FIRE**!

D'YOU REALIZE WHAT THIS MEANS....

I'VE BEEN LOOKING FOR A SMART BOY LIKE YOU!

GIMME A LIGHT!

"Watch out ... the plate's hot."

"I don't wanna be a juror!
Can't I be a witness?"

"It comes with a 5-year guarantee or
until you open the package,
whichever comes first."

"If you're sleep-walking toward the
fridge, leave the ham alone!"

"I guess we should have tried it on the rats first."

"Say when."

"I see you finally sewed on my button."

"Don't play with Grandpa's greasy hair just before suppertime."

"How does it feel to take some little kid's last dollar?"

"I'm your anesthetist and he's my back-up man."

"'F' means 'fantastic.'"

"Look what she did to my candy bar!"

"If I've got to tell the whole truth and nothing but the truth, what sort of fair trial is this gonna be?"

"Tomorrow I'm having you adopted."

"I only have one of those ... you can have it for half-price."

"Herman's a man of rare gifts. In 25 years, I've had one bunch of flowers."

"Four months, eight days, five hours and twenty minutes. Four months, eight days, five hours and nineteen minutes..."

"Slice of wedding cake?"

"The bank will lend you the money, but you have to prove to us that you don't really need it."

"That pain-in-the-neck's out here, doctor."

"Now what? There's nothing left to invent."

"Did you buy anything from him?"

"Well, when he comes back from lunch, tell him his war souvenir is making clicking noises."

"This watch you bought me is a great conversation piece. I have to ask everybody the time!"

"Columbus, will you sit down and stop asking all these dumb questions?"

"I'm NOT going camping. If you wanna get back to nature, take the screen off the window."

"'One Hundred and One Ways to Rip Off Credit Companies' ... is that cash or charge?"

"Don't forget to mark it 'Personal.'"

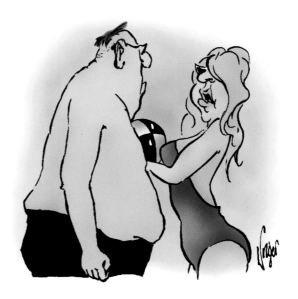

"Boy, Harry, you sure look different without your wallet!"

"I'm the babysitter. Where's the fridge?"

"I've changed my mind. I'll have
a cheese sandwich."

"Next time you go to the store, get
some proper paper napkins."

"When we say 'parents invited',
we usually mean to sit and watch."

HERMAN

JIM UNGER

I DON'T BELIEVE IT!

YOU'RE HAROLD! .... HAROLD SPRINGER.

NO!

YES YOU ARE! YOU'VE GOT A SISTER NAMED 'IVY'!

NO I HAVEN'T.

YOU USED TO LIVE ON MEADOW LANE!

NO

IMAGINE SEEING YOU AFTER ALL THESE YEARS!

HE'S NOTHING LIKE I REMEMBER HIM!

"You spotted it, eh?"

"What song did you sing?"

"Can I use your phone?"

"It looked smaller in the store!"

"I promise no more drilling if you let go."

"You're getting your knocks early,
Ralphy. ... Your car's being recalled."

"Your plane's been delayed ten minutes.
A couple of rivets popped loose."

"Here you go, 'Instant Leftovers.'"

"Saturday evenings with you are a real treat."

"It says: 'Come in Number 10, your hour is up.'"

"Chicken for breakfast, chicken for lunch, chicken for dinner. What d'you expect?"

"You can't be expected to get
it right the first time!"

"FIRED! Does that mean I won't
get the raise?"

"Why didn't you tell me your ex-boyfriend
was the guy who cuts my hair?"

"That's just his way of saying
he wants you to stay!"

"Hey, Harry! Look at this guy's wife."

"Okay, you've got five minutes
to capture my interest."

"Aren't you going to phone the airport?"

"Your boss says you can have the rest
of the afternoon off."

"Any other complaints?"

"I hope you used warm water.
I don't want to listen to those
things chattering all night."

"I'm trying to sleep. What have you got
up here – a performing elephant?"

"Size what?"

"Okay, who's next?"

"I'll be home soon; I'm at the Speedy
Shoe Repair Boutique."

"Thanks for phoning my boss for a raise.
Now guess why I don't have to set the
alarm clock for tomorrow morning."

"You can't claim a world record unless it sticks in the grass."

"Don't do that while I'm eating!"

"You've DEFINITELY got the flu."

"Pretend you're a purse snatcher; I wanna try something."

85

"What accident? I told you
I was making bookends."

"Just give it your best shot. I've got a
team of doctors standing by."

"D'you get the feeling one of us
is getting ripped-off?"

"Whaddya mean, 'Which one is ours?'"

"Grandpa, how do you change channels on this set?"

"You MUST have over-filled it!"

"He had to use the washroom, but he's never flown before."

"Did you say this pizza gave you indigestion?"

"There! Aren't you glad I made
you wear your seat belt?"

"Will you hurry up!"

"How sweet! A birthday card
mailed in 1986!"

"D'ya ever feel you're on the verge
of an incredible breakthrough?"

"Two of these just fell out of the car."

"I've got to go. Give my love
to everyone in Australia."

"Do you think the current economic
policies will do anything to ease
the unemployment situation?"

"This is my nephew. I want you to spend
the morning training him for your job."

"We'll take you off the vitamins
for a couple of days."

"I'm sure he'll be sorry he missed you."

"Why do I have to sit and look
at you everywhere we go?"

"What are the chances of me becoming a pirate?"

"This model comes with shoulder
straps for camping trips."

"I can't explain now, but don't take
your jacket off at work."

"What's my new sewing machine doing
in the middle of your poker game?"

"No, it's definitely not
the ON/OFF switch."

"Want me to get you a shopping cart?"

"What a stroke of luck – you being in the Army with the head waiter."

"You've got what we call 'heavy blood.'"

"Quit arguing and give him
the can opener."

"Hey, come and see this. There's a guy
who's been on strike for two years and
he can't remember where he works."

"That's not me, you idiot!"

"Okay Watson, come back inside.
You can have the afternoon off."

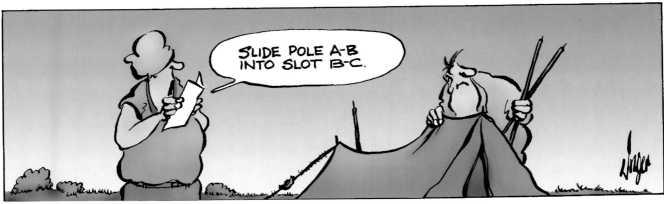

"This self-adjusting set is
giving me the creeps!"

"Five bucks if you start
practicing your violin."

"First weekend off in 10 years and
she wants to go canoeing!"

"Gimme the keys. Mom said
I could borrow the car."

"He's not allowed out so I bought
him a trampoline."

"Hey, I'm trying to watch television."

"He says it's no use.
He just has to do it."

"Tomorrow morning I want to see
you in my office."

"Okay, we need volunteers to play 'Beat the Croc.'"

"I think I'm gonna need to take a couple of sick days!"

"How about a 10 minute 'shore-leave' to take out the garbage?"

"Is that everything, just a bar of soap?"

"It's always the same when we go camping ... wakes up and can't remember where he is."

"I recommend the ketchup."

"HOLD IT."

"Mind if we play through?"

"I told you you planted that tree
too close to the house."

"Are you eating properly and getting
plenty of exercise?"

"This toaster's gotta go
back to the store!"

"You'd better get a good grip
on that net, Herman."

"My mother says either we get married
or I shouldn't see you anymore."

"Let me put it this way ...
for your weight you should be
thirty-seven feet tall."

"The museum does not require you to
wash the 5,000 year old jugs, Agnes."

"She gets nervous when we use
the new dishes."

102

"D'you realize we've been out for four hours and we're not even on the third green?"

"If you're going to wear that coat, I think you could use a lighter shade."

"Commander, how does it feel to be back on Earth after six months of weightlessness?"

"I told you it was a big sand-trap."

"Who's going to have their injection?"

"Onions ... garlic ... they look
the same to me."

"If she has one more birthday, this
whole place is gonna go up!"

HERMAN

JIM

DIDN'T I ASK THAT WAITER FOR WHITE BREAD?

WE RAN OUT OF PEA SOUP, SO I BROUGHT YOU CHICKEN NOODLE.

HEY! WHERE'S MY BAKED POTATO?

IT'S NINE O'CLOCK! WE ONLY HAVE FRENCH FRIES LEFT....

WAITER... I'LL HAVE THE CHECK.

THIRTY-NINE DOLLARS.

HERE ARE TWO FIVES. I RAN OUT OF TWENTIES.

"I don't care if you did miss
the last bus. ... GET OFF."

"Here, don't touch the stick."

"Imagine if I walked around
dressed like that!"

"I don't think I'll bother with
a tan 'til I get out."

106

"Did you knock?"

"I'm getting sick of watching that water cooler go past my office at ten minutes past nine every morning."

"If we don't need any brushes, you come and tell this guy!"

"I've got a terrible headache. I think I'm gonna make an example of you."

"Why don't you buy a proper set of headphones?"

"Whaddya mean the pointer-arm's broken off!"

"Herman's so considerate when I'm sick. ... He dragged the washer and dryer up to the bedroom."

"I called earlier but your wife said you hadn't got the intelligence to read these books."

"If you'd read the instructions, you'd see there's one switch for drying and another for styling."

"Let me see those gloves."

"Imagine those crooks wanting eleven bucks to fix this!"

"You've been in business 40 years
and you don't take credit cards?!"

"I'll give you two clues ... the cat's
missing and we get an animal show
on every channel."

"Don't go too far tonight –
you'll miss 'Seinfeld.'"

"Forgive the intrusion, but I wonder
if you'd mind telling the janitor
the elevator's stuck?"

"Want me to make a little hole
and feed you some grapes?"

"Don't worry, this'll probably
hurt me more than you."

"Nice work, George. You've injured
his right arm."

"I know he's got big feet but
you haven't seen him swim."

"Okay, take a break!"

"How do you want your eggs ...
black or dark brown?"

"Normally I ignore things said to me in
fun at the Christmas party, however ..."

"Take your foot off the stupid brake!"

"I suppose you realize your
alarm clock didn't go off and
you're an hour late for work?"

"The cat went berserk!"

"Why don't you throw it at
the one who cooks it?"

"Take it easy with him —
his wife just had triplets."

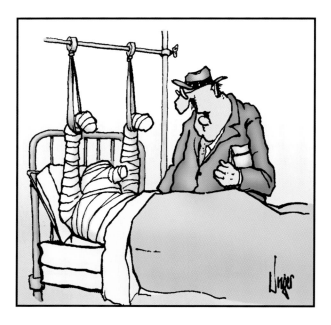

"You're looking a lot
better today, Ralph."

"Two weeks of jogging and so far
he's made it to the front door."

"He opened all the windows halfway
through the car wash."

"Whaddya mean, 'nothing to do'?
Who do you think defrosts the fridge?"

"There, let's see a burglar get past him!"

"Go across the square, pass the nurse's residence, up the steps, through the main lobby and second door on your left."

"You getting athlete's foot is about as ridiculous as a coal miner with sunstroke!"

"Why do you always decide to take a bath just when supper's ready?"

"Now don't start practicing until Daddy
gets down the road a ways, and I'll pick
you up in two hours."

"Can you remember where
I bought this suit?"

"Look in my sister's blue bag."

"And you wonder why I never want
to go to Italian restaurants!"

"I appreciate you've got a wife and six kids but you can't wash apartment windows in that rig."

"Okay ... here are the results of your medical."

"All bets are off if you don't quit laughing."

"Father, I cannot tell a lie. ... George Washington did it."

"Why take a week off? You've got time to get married and have a honeymoon on one of your coffee breaks."

"What are the chances of time off for good behavior?"

"I know it's sudden, but I want a divorce!"

"I'd better warn you. If my grades don't start improving, one of us won't be getting a new bike for Christmas."

"STAY!"

"Don't sit on the beanbag chair –
it's got a split in it."

"That's in case you lose your door key."

"Isn't it time he went to bed?"

"I sometimes wonder if you hear
one word I say!"

"I thought you liked it strong."

"I thought your doctor told you to get away and RELAX."

"It was supposed to be Mom, but I messed it up."

"It's done wonders for his self-confidence since we had his teeth capped."

"A-B-C-E … G."

"I don't care if you are the boss.
You tell him!"

"Here, eat as fast as you can. I have
some big tippers waiting for this table."

"How come I never get a copy
of the script?"

"His English teacher says he's
a really awesome dude."

"Just half your money …
I got an arrangement with the guy
in the next bush!"

"I just spent $8,000 having
this room soundproofed."

"As soon as my arms get tired, I'll come
down and you can have a go."

"Will that do?"

"You're fighting the King in
the semi-finals, so just duck once
and he won't get too tired."

"There! It fits like a glove when
you stand up straight."

"When everyone is supposed to be
conserving energy ... you're certainly
doing your bit."

"Oh no! Is there another word
I can use instead of 'verily' that
starts with a 'B?'"

"Nice try!"

"Why don't you just go to
a proper dentist?"

"You must have run a mile this time –
you've been gone four minutes."

"Don't take any notice. ... He's trying to quit smoking."

"You wouldn't believe the terrible time I have getting him out of bed in the morning."

"Even as a kid I was a slow eater."

"I think it represents man's eternal struggle for freedom."

"Allow me to introduce myself. ...
I'm a basketball talent scout."

"Why did you ruin the tiger
trap he made?"

"He's doing two week's 'solitary!'"

"This is your last chance. If you scalp
this one, you're through."

"I know it's your first day, but you've got to accept the fact that some customers are just 'lookers.'"

"Yeah? Well if people look like their pets, why don't you go home and look after your gorilla?"

"If you've got any screaming to do, wait until you leave the premises."

"I don't know what species it is, but my instincts tell me that we should be about forty miles away when it hatches."

"He's allergic to carrots."

"Okay that's it ... that's the last time
he watches a martial arts movie."

"How would you like to eat
off the floor every day?"

"We're not gonna charge you
for this first lesson."

"I think it's the TV repairman."

"Did you forget to water my plants while I was away?"

"Now, imagine you've cornered a bear and he runs in to an abandoned house."

"What was that?"

"Suppose we decide not to watch one night. Do you remember how to switch it off?"

"My mistake! I thought I heard
a noise down here."

"Whaddya think, Ma, eighty-five bucks?"

"Maybe next time you'll think twice
about losing your key."

"Start? Start what? I thought you said
you hired me to take care of the books."

"Don't you want your receipt?"

"This looks good ... 'Mailman flavored.'"

"They've cured my arthritis!"

"My 'secrets of life' are now available
on CD for only $26.95."

"This is Blue Buzzard, good buddy;
Smokey's on the warpath."

"You're looking at it upside down!"

"Ask him if he ever heard of a tortoise
having a heart attack."

"Don't go rushing into marriage.
Look around for a couple of years
like your mother did."

"Who's calling? D'you know
what time it is?"

"Testing ... testing ... one, two, three."

"Can't you sit still for five minutes? Whaddya want my camera for now?"

"Will you quit shouting 'land on the starboard beam,' while we're in port!"

"Has he had his dinner?"

"What did he mean, 'love is blind?'"

"QUIT SHOVING!"

"Did you feel the earthquake?"

"Have I got time for a cup of coffee?"

"You're using my athlete's foot ointment."

"I may as well tell you, that's the last one we've got in your size."

"I paid $20 for it and it
hasn't rung once!"

"I GOT A HOLE-IN-ONE!"

"You've got Egyptian flu. You're
going to be a 'mummy.'"

"The results of all your tests
were negative. Get lost!"

"I told him he needed more feathers."

"Er, Doc ... can he have a quick look at your diploma?"

"How many times have I told you to wear your helmet?"

"Hey, Michelangelo ... I thought I said two coats of oyster white for the ceiling."

"Why can't you dry your feet with a towel like everybody else?"

"That was a good idea, sending out for pizza while the elevator's on the fritz."

"I wish you wouldn't talk about buying a dog when he's listening."

"If I can't get a summer job this year, I think I'll get married."

"Listen, if you want to eat in the office BRING SANDWICHES!"

"I can't get a cab – we'll have to take the bus!"

"Have you ever known a day to drag on like this?"

"Try to imagine how much I care!"

"Try to relax ... he can smell fear."

"Grannie's leg just fell off!"

"It just says, 'Windows repaired
– five bucks.'"

"If you want a concise, professional
opinion: You're as nutty as a fruitcake."

"Do we need a set of encyclopedias?"

"Herman, I can see perfectly well without a chair to stand on ... Herman!!!"

"You've got to start sometime. Why don't you operate on this one?"

"I won't be in to work today, my wife's sick!"

"Listen, I gotta go. There's a guy waiting to use the phone."

"Next door wants 'The Blue Danube.'"

"I've got two other applicants to see before I make my final choice."

"Whadya mean, you wanna marry my daughter? I thought you were my daughter!"

"If I don't get a raise soon, I'm gonna blow the lid off this crummy zoo."

"He's a self-made man."

"Stop complaining. How often does she get to see a drive-in movie?"

"I'll never forget the time you strapped me for talking in class."

"You know, a brain like yours is wasted cutting weeds."

"Psst, boss. I guess this is not a good time to ask for a raise, huh?"

"That's the second time you've fallen asleep in the bath with your mouth open."

"Well, if we can't cure it, you can always get a job in a restaurant."

"Why don't you wear long socks 'til he learns to tell the difference between your leg and a bone?"

"According to this, you've been having a back problem."

"I make it three million shopping days to Christmas."

"Listen, if we get this right, we'll be famous."

"Why don't you buy it? ... It obviously likes you."

"It's nothing personal, Harold, but you make me sick and I never want to see you again."

"I really look forward to your cheery little visits."

"One more 'Olé!' and you can cut the grass yourself."

"I thought you said you had experience in this type of work."

"Did you shake the bottle?"

"Boy! You sure know how to break a vow of silence."

"One seat in the front and one seat in the back."

"Well, now we know what all that squawking was about last night."

"I told you I was smart. My teacher says she's given up trying to teach me anything."

"Two hundred million years ago, it ate insects."

"I warned you about iron tonic. Your stomach's rusty."

"Would it help any if I started sending your alimony weekly?"

"Will you stop complaining?! You're the one who didn't want separate vacations."

"Don't be such a miser! Take him on the Rocket Ride again."

"He's kicking my seat again. I thought you were going to say something?"

"I hope it's not inconvenient.
We're your new neighbors."

"He's getting better. He can remember
everything now except getting married."

"Take your boots off.
I just scrubbed the floor."

"Wake up, Daddy."

"Memorize this. It's your New Year resolutions."

"It's a guy called Christopher Columbus ... it's okay, he's only staying a couple of hours."

"If I'd known you were coming I'd have got a job."

"Me and the boys were trying to guess how you spell your name."

"We'll take a brief pause for this important commercial message."

"Sorry!"

"Now, Polly, let Mr. Herman
finish his coffee."

"Look at this ... Mexican Curry
for two dollars."

"Couldn't resist, could you?"

"All the clocks have stopped!"

"There's nothing in my contract about
picking up your lunch order
on the way back here."

"Members of the jury, have you
reached a verdict?"

"Come and see what he's invented
– a clock that doesn't need electricity."

HERMAN

JIM Unger

TABLE FOR ONE, SIR?

D'YOU NEED ANYONE TO WASH DISHES?

WE'RE FULLY STAFFED.

I COULD CLEAN TABLES OR MAYBE DO A SPOT OF COOKING...

WILL YOU PUSH OFF!

YOU HAVE A RESERVATION FOR SEVEN O'CLOCK..

...FOURTEEN PEOPLE, NAME OF PARKER...

SO WHAT!

WE WON'T BE COMING.

"I can assure you I wake up
at the slightest sound."

"This TV dinner's got wires in it!"

"Take that cereal out in the yard 'til it
stops snapping and crackling."

"Now don't tell me your old vacuum
cleaner can do that."

"If you help him with his homework, at least we won't have to worry about college fees."

"See that?! I forgot to tighten the nut."

"Come along, dear. Grandpa never was very musical."

"If you remember, I did mention possible side-effects."

"Relax, I've come to fix the window."

"Just you start something.
My husband's a karate expert."

"How come God put all the vitamins
in cabbage and nothing in candy?"

"I'm giving thanks for hamburger.
Give me half a pound."

"I'll come back later when you're not busy."

"Your mother warned me you'd start complaining about your food."

"Nothing to declare."

"I thought you told me we didn't give 'cash refunds.'"

"Don't look at me like that. He chose it!"

"I hate to disturb you at mealtime,
but can I borrow a cup of sugar?"

"This is the latest vegetable
slicer from France."

"Try to guess who this is for."

"I know it's three o'clock in the morning but I wanted to tell you how much I'm enjoying the singing."

"You're washing the floor with the soup-of-the-day!"

"Don't blame me. I was cleaning his cage and he flew up the pipe."

"Is there anything you need before I go?"

"Let's face it; if you'd really loved me,
you'd have married someone else!"

"You're my last hope, Harry. Can
I borrow your dinner jacket?"

"It's the cook's coffee-break, so eat
your dessert first."

"Had any luck?"

"Is that your idea of cutting down
to two cigarettes a day?"

"You know, if you keep telling me
about birds and bees, I'm gonna
lose interest in girls."

"Smarten up! Sometimes I think your
father's got more brains than you have."

"If I think it's going to a good home,
you can have it for twelve bucks."

"For the tenth time, I'm NOT
going bowling."

"Next."

"You've got an hour to paint your
nails and talk to your mother.
I'm going to a meeting."

"I thought you said you were coming
home next Sunday."

"How could anyone sit
on a welding torch?"

"Debbie looks exactly like me
when I was 18."

"Just as I thought ... you need
a new picture tube!"

"Of course I care for you. Money and
looks aren't everything, you know!"

"I can always tell when they're
wearing 'elevator shoes.'"

"Good morning."

"Whaddya mean 'checkmate'?
Get to bed."

"Keep in mind you're a guest
on this bench."

"Why don't you let your husband
go to the ball game?"

"A truck ran over my cast!"

"I know you're in bed with the flu, but I
need the keys to the filing cabinet."

"He thinks we're muggers!"

"I think I'll sell all my jewelry.
I need the five dollars."

"D'you take plastic?"

"This is my first day. Do we get paid?"

"I thought while I was getting the fuses,
I'd pick up a few groceries."

"OK class ... name four things he did wrong."

"I don't care how much he likes Flipper,
I wanna watch baseball."

"D'you like that blue?"

"Let's face it, Stella, we've grown apart.
We need two televisions!"

"He's due for his annual shots."

"You ever thought of selling this recipe to the Pentagon?"

"How long have you had your feet on the wrong legs?"

"Hope it's not too dry."

"I plugged it in to see if you'd fixed it."

"What would you give someone who's
giving you a bowling ball?"

"Come on, Dad, it's over!"

"I thought I'd put in a little
vegetable garden."

"Well, someone phoned in an order
for five pounds of peanuts."

"Look on the bright side. You've still got your new captain's hat."

"If you're gonna do yoga every night,
I want my own TV."

"Did it ever cross your mind that maybe
you're being out-smarted by a mouse?"

"You park the car, I'm going to bed."

"Fifteen years is not so long.
You've already done 12 days."

"Maybe you're beginning to get the message that we need a recreation room."

"Last Christmas, I asked my wife to smuggle a file into the prison."

"He had his heart set on a cowboy suit."

"Going up the Amazon?"

"It'll take you a couple of days to get used to these express elevators."

"I cut a piece off the bottom and patched your shirt."

"Is it okay to leave if I lose all my money?"

"Well, well ... My secret file tells me that this is your grandmother's seventh funeral since 1975."

"Missed!"

"Now whatever happens, hang on to those sandwiches!"